Our SPECIAL World

THE SEASONS

Liz Lennon

W

FRANKLIN WATTS
LONDON·SYDNEY

Contents

Franklin Watts
First published in Great Britain in 2016 by
The Watts Publishing Group

Copyright © The Watts Publishing Group, 2016
All rights reserved.

Series Editor: Sarah Peutrill   Editor: Sarah Ridley
Consultant: Karina Philip   Designer: Will Dawes
Cover Designer: Cathryn Gilbert

HB ISBN: 978 1 4451 4902 8
PB ISBN: 978 1 4451 4904 2
Printed in China

Franklin Watts
An imprint of
Hachette Children's Group
Part of The Watts Publishing Group
Carmelite House
50 Victoria Embankment
London EC4Y 0DZ

An Hachette UK Company
www.hachette.co.uk
www.franklinwatts.co.uk

FSC
www.fsc.org
MIX
Paper from
responsible sources
FSC® C104740

Picture credits: agefotostock/Alamy: 14t; Blend Images/Alamy: 13t, 13b, 24bc; Blickwinkel/Alamy: 16t; BlueOrangeStudio/Shutterstock: 12b; Jennie Bowden/Dreamstime: front cover cl, 3tc; David Cole/Alamy: 18b, 24tl; Daxiao Productions/Shutterstock: 1, 7t; Sharon Day/Shutterstock: 19t; Design Pics Inc/Alamy: 4, 24cl; Designsstock/Shutterstock: 7cl; Mikhail Dudarev/Shutterstock: 8-9, 24c; Ron Edwards/Alamy: 5b; Juergen Faelchle/Shuttrstock: 18t; Geophotos/Alamy: 17b; Tatyana Gladskikh/Dreamstime: front cover l, 3tr; Gotzila Freedom/Shutterstock: 22cr; Jamie Grill/Alamy: 5t; Peter Henrie/Alamy: 10b; Hoxton/Alamy: 8b; Incamerastock/Alamy: 14b, 24br; Artem Kasparyan/Shutterstock: 7br; koi88/Alamy: 15t; Denis Kuvaiev/Dreamstime: front cover r, 3b; Loop Images/Alamy: 6b; Terry Matthews/Alamy: 10t, 24tr; maxpro/Shutterstock: 7bl; MNStudio/Shutterstock: 15c, 24bl; Monkey Business/Shutterstock: 21b; Nadezhda1906/Shutterstock: 20b; Dmitry Naumov/Dreamstime: front cover cr; Pixelbliss/Shutterstock: 7cr; Plantology/Alamy: 15b, 24tc; RF Company/Alamy: 6t, 24cr; Salsa/Alamy: 20t; spass/Shutterstock: 3tl; Rita Storey/Franklin Watts 21t, 22bl, 23; 3445128471/Shutterstock: 11; Colin Varndell/Alamy: 19b; Jaren Jai Wicklund/Shutterstock: 12t; wildlife gmbk/Alamy: 16b, 17t.

Every attempt has been made to clear copyright. Should there be any inadvertent omission please apply to the publisher for rectification.

Four seasons

There are four seasons in the year.

? ? ?

Can you name each season?

Spring

As winter ends, the weather warms up and there is more daylight. Spring has arrived!

Many animals have their young in spring. Here is a sheep with her lamb.

Which animals have their young in spring?

Trees and plants grow new shoots and leaves.

Spring flowers bring colour to parks and gardens.

Summer

In summer it gets even warmer. The days are longer and there is more sunshine.

Meadows and gardens fill with summer flowers.

The warm sunshine helps crops to grow.

It is fun to be outside in summer.

What are your favourite summer foods?

Autumn

In autumn the days get shorter and colder. Some trees lose their leaves and drop their seeds.

It's fun to kick the leaves on the ground!

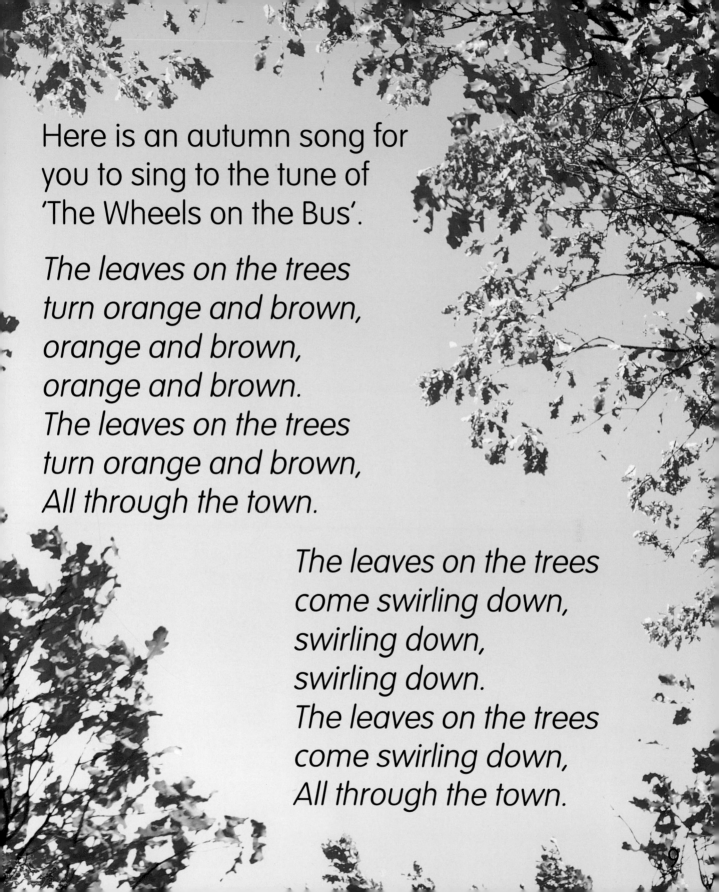

Here is an autumn song for you to sing to the tune of 'The Wheels on the Bus'.

*The leaves on the trees
turn orange and brown,
orange and brown,
orange and brown.
The leaves on the trees
turn orange and brown,
All through the town.*

*The leaves on the trees
come swirling down,
swirling down,
swirling down.
The leaves on the trees
come swirling down,
All through the town.*

Winter

In winter the days are short. It's colder outside and it snows in some places.

On very cold days, everything is covered in frost.

Some animals grow thicker fur to keep warm.

Liam is choosing some winter words.
Which words would you choose?

scarf

frost

cold

snow

gloves

sneeze

ice

coat

dark

fire

chilly

Seasonal clothes

We wear clothes to match the seasons.

Davey's family are dressed for a spring walk.

Freddie and Lucy are at the beach in summer.

Jack is collecting autumn leaves.

What are the children wearing in each picture?

Lily is wrapped up warm to make a snowman.

Plants and the seasons

We see different plants in each season.

In spring
we can see
woodland
flowers.

Sunflowers grow tall
in the summer
sunshine.

Juicy strawberries are ready to eat in summer.

In autumn orange pumpkins are ready to pick.

There are fewer flowers in winter. Do you know the name of this one?

The answer is on page 24.

Trees

Here are four photos of apple trees. Can you match the right season to each tree?

spring   summer

autumn   winter

a

b

c

d

The answers are on page 24.

Animal changes

The seasons affect animals too.

In spring birds build nests and lay eggs. Bees feed on nectar in blossom and flowers.

In spring and summer, animals care for their young. Birds find insects to feed to their chicks.

In autumn some birds fly away to warmer places. Other animals search for food to store for winter.

In winter there is less food for animals to eat. Dormice go to sleep to survive winter.

Seasonal fun

We can have fun outside all year around.

Spring days can be windy. Josh is flying his kite!

Ice skating is fun to try in winter.

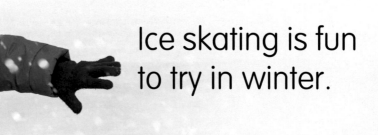

Ooooops!

Art ideas

Here are some ideas for seasonal art.

Summer or autumn
Put a leaf on a flat surface.
Cover it with a piece of white paper.

Rub a crayon on the paper
to make a leaf rubbing.

Spring
Luke made this daffodil. What did he use to make it?

What ideas have you got for a winter art project?

Word bank

 Chicks

 Flowers

 Frost

 Lamb

 Leaves

 Meadow

 Pumpkin

 Snowman

 Sunflowers

Index

Answers to the questions: page 15: snowdrops; pages 16 and 17: a – autumn, b - spring, c - summer, d - winter.